Birds in the Sky

Dedication

Birds In The Sky, Mama Rama edition is dedicated to Rahmatoullahy Barry Mahotiere, wife to Dr. Sauveur mahotiere and mother to Sauveur Mahotiere Jr., Algassim Barry Mahotiere and Malon Mahotiere.

About the Author

Malon Mahotiere is a business owner, barber and licensed Master Cosmetologist. Malon became an entrepreneur when she was 7 years old. She started by selling glitter pencils to her friends. When Malon turned 17, she decided to become a Hair Stylist. Malon started her first business at age 22. She later started 2 more businesses. She has attended several schools for education and training to expand her knowledge. Malon is a U.S. Air Force Veteran, Beauty Coach and creative artist. She enjoys spending her time exercising and singing.

Prologue

Birds in the Sky is a self-help book to inspire children who are grieving the loss of one or both parents. This book is designed for children of all ages, starting from age 1. Birds in the Sky tells the story of 3 African American children who lost both of their parents in a fatal car accident. These children survived the accident. However, they were left in this world without proper guidance. Each child developed into adulthood, struggling with grief and identity issues. This book helps teach children about the stages of grief, empathy, and self-acceptance. The birds in the sky represent the guardian angels of a departed loved one.

Poem

Your love is so dear because it is always near. I don't have to cry because I know you are near-by. When times get hard, I stare at the stars. In the sunlight, I see you afar.

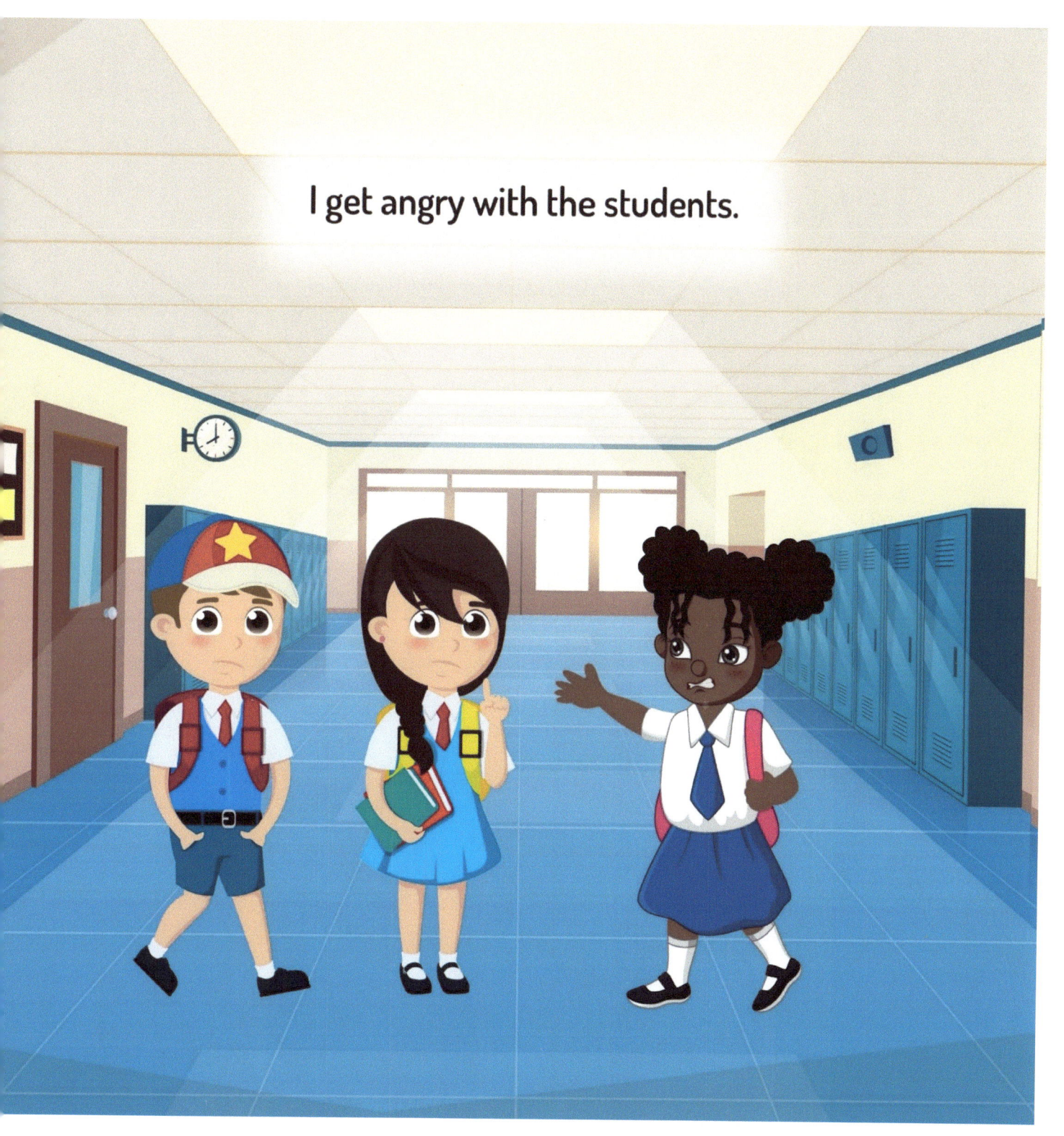

Mama Rama says, "You don't have to look. I'm always with you. If you can't see me, please know I am there. If you really want to see, look at the sky. Keep your head up there.

THE END

www.ingramcontent.com/pod-product-compliance
Lightning Source LLC
Chambersburg PA
CBHW042125040426
42450CB00002B/77